A New True Book

FOOTBALL

By Ray Broekel

Children's Press®
A Division of Grolier Publishing
New York   London   Hong Kong   Sydney
Danbury, Connecticut

PHOTO CREDITS

AllSport — © Rick Stewart, cover, 30 (left), 39 (top); © Tony Duffy, 4 (bottom); © Ken Levine, 7; © Doug Pensinger, 11 (top); © Jonathan Daniel, 12, 38 (center); © Stephen Dunn, 15, 25, 26, 42; © Mike Powell, 20 (top), 21, 29, 30 (top right), 37, 38 (bottom), 39 (center); © Jeff Gossett, 23 (left); © Simon Bruty, 23 (right); © T. Rosenberg, 35; © Otto Greule, 38 (top); © Ron Chenoy, 41

AP/ Wide World — 17 (bottom 2 photos), 19, 20

Unicorn Stock Photos — © Martin R. Jones, 2; © Robert W. Ginn, 4 (top); © Eric R. Berndt, 9; © Mike Morris, 11 (bottom), 17 (top), 39 (bottom); © Dick Young, 30 (bottom); © Aneal Vohra, 31

Cover — The Philadelphia Eagles vs. the Washington Redskins

Library of Congress Cataloging-in-Publication Data

Broekel, Ray.
  Football / by Ray Broekel.
     p. cm. — (A new true book)
  Includes index.
  Summary: Describes the game of football as it is played by high school, college, and professional teams and lists the teams and some famous players of the National Football League.
  ISBN 0-516-01082-4
  1. Football — Juvenile literature. [1. Football.] I. Title.
GV950.7.875 1995
796.332'2 — dc20   95-16451
                                                    CIP   AC

CONTENTS

Some boys play on football teams when they are eight and nine years old. They continue playing in elementary school, high school, and college.

THE HISTORY OF FOOTBALL

In the United States, football is played on many levels — elementary, high-school, college, and professional. Each has its own rules.

Football in the United States began in the mid-1800s as a version of two English kicking games — soccer and rugby. At first, football was a college game. Then, it was played in high schools.

Not until the 1890s was football played professionally.

In 1920, eleven clubs formed the American Professional Football Association in Canton, Ohio. Later, it changed its name to the National Football League.

Georgia Dome — the Falcolns stadium in Atlanta, Georgia

THE PLAYING FIELD

A football field is called a "gridiron." It is 120 yards long. Its surface may be natural grass or artificial turf. It can be in an indoor or outdoor stadium.

There are goal lines at each end of the field. The distance between the two goal lines is 100 yards.

Ten yards beyond the goal lines are the goal posts. The space between the goal posts and the goal lines is the end zone.

The field has white lines every five yards. These lines are called yard lines. The 50-yard line is called midfield.

The 50-yard line is in the center of the field.

During a game, eleven players on each side defend their end zone by stopping the other side from scoring.

EQUIPMENT

Football players wear tight-fitting jerseys and pants. This makes it difficult to grab and tackle them. They wear shoes with cleats so that they can run well on grass or artificial turf.

Players' helmets are made of hard plastic. The helmet are held in place with a chin

Cleats on the bottom of players' shoes are made of hard rubber or plastic.

Players wear different masks on their helmets for safety.

11

guard. In front of the helmet is a face mask. Each player wears a mouthpiece to protect his teeth.

Shoulder pads, which prevent injuries, are worn by all players.

Pads are worn under the jerseys and pants. All players wear shoulder pads, hip pads, thigh pads, and knee pads. Some wear elbow pads and rib pads, too.

A football is made of leather. It is about 11 inches long and 7 inches wide at its center. It weighs between 14 and 15 ounces. There are leather laces along one side of the ball. The laces help a player to grip the ball.

THE OFFENSIVE TEAM

The team with the ball is the offensive team. It tries to move the ball across the other team's goal line to score.

The offensive team must go forward at least ten yards in four plays, or downs. If it cannot, it must give the ball to the other team.

It gives the ball to the other team by punting, or

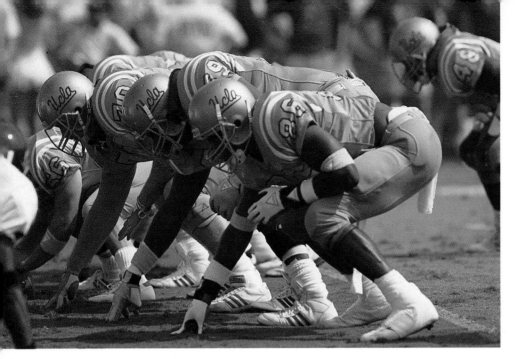

University of California at Los Angeles (UCLA)
offensive line

kicking, it to them on the
fourth down.

If the team moves forward
ten yards or more, it gets a
first down. Then it has four
more chances to move the
ball ten yards.

The quarterback leads the offensive team. He calls the plays in huddles. He hands the ball off to a running back or throws a pass to a receiver. Sometimes, the quarterback runs with the ball himself.

Other players on the offensive team are called linemen. They block and tackle the other team's players. They try to keep them from tackling the man with the ball.

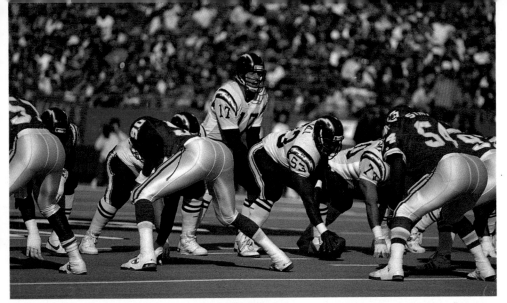

Top: A quarterback gives the call to snap the ball and begin play. Bottom: A quarterback can throw a pass (left) or keep the ball (right) and run with it .

THE DEFENSIVE TEAM

The team without the ball is the defensive team. It tries to keep the offensive team from moving the ball forward.

A defensive player can tackle the man with the ball. He can block a pass. He can catch, or intercept, a pass. He can get the ball if it is dropped, or fumbled.

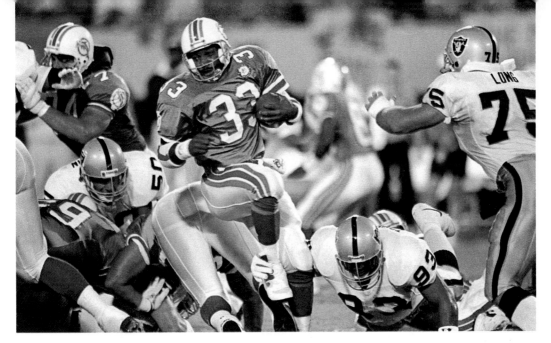

On the offense, Miami Dolphins running back struggles to gain yards. Los Angeles Raiders defense holds him back.

Some defensive players are called linemen. They start each play facing the other team. They try to tackle the person carrying the ball. If they tackle the quarterback before he can throw the ball, it is called a "sack."

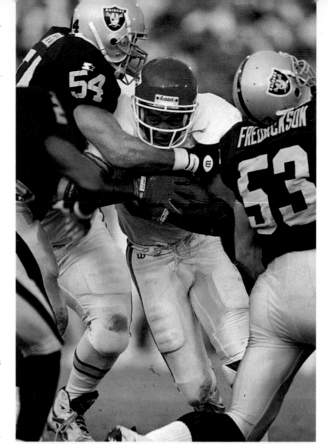

Top: Raiders defensive linemen stop Kansas City Chiefs Marcus Allen from advancing the ball. Bottom: Raiders defensive lineman Anthony Smith blocks a pass by Seattle Seahawks quarterback Dave Krieg.

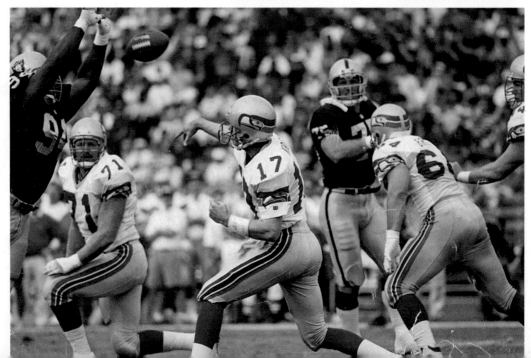

Pittsburgh Steelers player stretches to intercept a pass thrown to Dallas Cowboys Michael Irvin.

The players behind linemen are called linebackers. They stand 2 or 3 yards behind them. They try to intercept, or catch, passes thrown by the other team's quarterback. Linebackers must be quick. They have to catch the ball carrier and tackle him.

THE SPECIAL TEAM

    Besides offensive and defensive players on a football team, there are also players on special teams, or kicking teams.

    These players are on the field for punts, kick-offs, field-goal attempts, and extra points after touchdowns.

Punting (left) and power blocking
(right) are both jobs of special teams.

The work of special
teams is rough. Players
have to be big and fast
and tough.

23

SCORING

A team scores points in four ways. A touchdown is six points. To score a touchdown, a team moves the ball across the other team's goal line.

After a touchdown, the scoring team has one play to make extra points. It can kick the ball through

San Diego Chargers Natrone Means lunges for a touchdown.

the goal posts for one
extra point. Or, it can run
or pass the ball into the
end zone for two points.

A teammate, sometimes a quarterback, holds the ball for the kicker when he attempts a field goal or a point after touchdown.

If a team cannot score a touchdown, it tries for a field goal. A field goal is three points. It is scored when the ball is kicked between the goal posts.

Sometimes a player is caught with the ball in his team's end zone. If the other team tackles him there, it scores a safety. A safety is two points.

THE OFFICIALS

Sometimes a player breaks a rule. He commits a foul. When that happens, the officials give his team a penalty. Usually his team loses yards. Sometimes it will lose a down, or play.

Officials use signals to show what kind of foul a player has made.

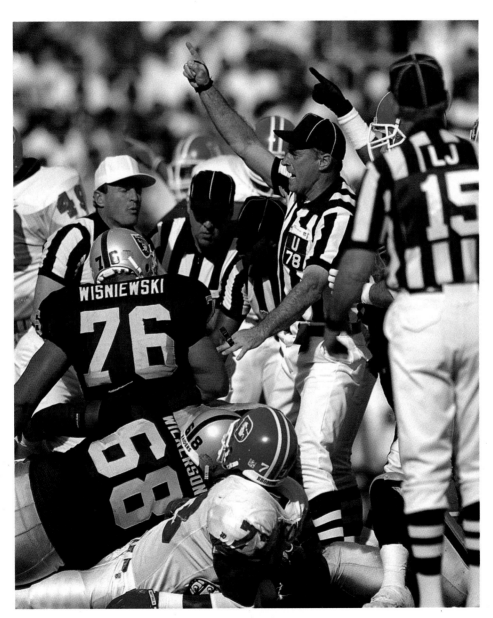

The umpire gives the final ruling on a play.

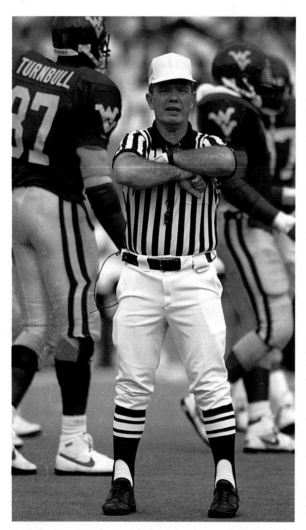

An official's hand signals can indicate a delay of game (top left), a time out (top right), or a touchdown, successful field goal, or successful extra point (bottom).

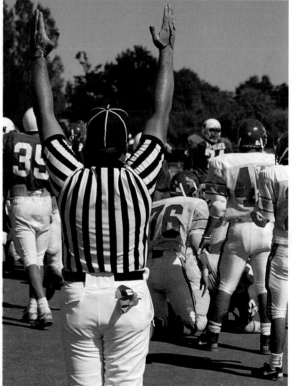

30

Seven officials supervise a pro football game. The referee is the head official. He gives the final ruling.

The umpire watches for violations at the lines of scrimmage—the imaginary lines where the offensive and defensive teams face each other.

An official carefully watches the play at the line of scrimmage.

The head linesman
watches the ball move up
and down the field. He
keeps track of the downs.

The line judge is in
charge of timing the
game. He supervises the
scoreboard clock. He
fires the pistol that ends
each half of the game.

The field judge watches
for violations on punt
plays and deep passes.
He also decides if the

field-goal and extra-point attempts are good.

The back judge watches for violations involved in catching the ball. He makes out-of-bounds rulings on his side of the field and also decides if the field-goal and extra-point attempts are good.

The side judge has the same responsibilities as the back judge, but on the opposite side of the field.

PLAYING TIME

In professional and college football, the ball is in play for 60 minutes. In high-school games, it is in play for 48 minutes.

However, games actually last much longer, because the game clock is stopped after scoring, and when a ball carrier goes out of bounds. The clock is also

A scoreboard shows the Green Bay Packers 10 to 0 lead over the Minnesota Vikings. Can you tell what quarter it is and the remaining time of play?

stopped when there are incomplete passes, time-outs, injuries, or penalties.

There is another reason game play can be stopped. When a game is on television, it is interrupted to show commercials.

A game is divided into two halves. Each half is made up of two quarters, or periods.

Teams can take three time-outs each half. Also, they can leave the field to take a fifteen minute rest in between halves. This is called halftime.

THE NATIONAL FOOTBALL LEAGUE

The National Football League has 28 teams grouped into two conferences. Each conference has three divisions.

National Football Conference

Eastern Division

Dallas Cowboys
New York Giants
Philadelphia Eagles
Phoenix Cardinals
Washington Redskins

Troy Aikman,
Denver Cowboys

Central Division

Chicago Bears
Detroit Lions
Green Bay Packers
Minnesota Vikings
Tampa Bay Buccaneers

Barry Sanders,
Detroit Lions

Western Division

Atlanta Falcons
St. Louis Rams
New Orleans Saints
San Francisco 49ers

Steve Young,
San Francisco 49ers

American Football Conference

Eastern Division
Buffalo Bills
Indianapolis Colts
Miami Dolphins
New England Patriots
New York Jets

Thomas Smith,
Buffalo Bills

Central Division
Cincinnati Bengals
Cleveland Browns
Houston Oilers
Pittsburgh Steelers

Pittsburg Steelers

Western Division
Denver Broncos
Kansas City Chiefs
Los Angeles Raiders
San Diego Chargers
Seattle Seahawks

Steve Deberg,
Kansas City Chiefs

THE SUPER BOWL

During the regular season, each pro team plays sixteen games. At the end of the season, the team that wins the championship of its division and other "wildcard" teams advance to playoff games. The two winners become conference champions

In Super Bowl XXVI, the Washington Redskins defeated the Buffalo Bills 37-24.

and meet in the Super Bowl. The team that wins the Super Bowl becomes the NFL champion.

Famous Professional Players

Troy Aikman, Dallas Cowboys

George Blanda, Chicago Bears, Baltimore Colts, Houston Oilers, Oakland Raiders

Terry Bradshaw, Pittsburgh Steelers

Jim Brown, Cleveland Browns

Dick Butkus, Chicago Bears

Dan Marino, Miami Dolphins

Joe Montana, San Francisco 49ers, Kansas City Chiefs

Joe Namath, New York Jets

Walter Payton, Chicago Bears

Jerry Rice, San Francisco 49ers

Gale Sayers, Chicago Bears

O.J. Simpson, Buffalo Bills

Bart Starr, Green Bay Packers

Roger Staubach, Dallas Cowboys

Jim Thorpe, Canton Bulldogs

Johnny Unitas, Baltimore Colts

Jerry Rice, San Francisco 49ers

GLOSSARY

artificial (ar te fĭsh'el) — not natural; made by people

block (blŏk) — to keep players from getting the ball

champion (chăm' pē en) — the winner; the best

commercial (că mur' shăl) — an advertisement on radio or television

conversion (kun vur'shen) — in football, the act of making an extra point after a touchdown, by kicking the football between the goal posts

defense (dē' fence) — the team that does not have the ball

down — a football play in which a team tries to move the ball forward

end zone — the space between the goal posts and the goal line

field goal (fēld gōl) — three points, scored by kicking the ball between the goal posts

foul — to break a rule

fumble — to drop the ball

gridiron (grĭd´ ī ern) — a football field

huddle (hŭd´ l) — players grouped around a quarterback to determine a play of action

imaginary (ĭ măg´ ĕ nĕrē) — not real; made up

intercept (ĭn ter sĕpt´) — to catch the ball when it is passed by a player on the other team

league (lēg) — a group of teams divided into two conferences

midfield (mĭd fēld) — the middle of a football field; the 50-yard line

offense (off´ ence) — the team that has the ball and is trying to score

official (ō fish´ el) the person who is in charge

penalty (pĕn´ el tē) — to lose yards or a down because a player breaks the rule

punt (punt) — to drop the ball and kick it before it hits the ground

referee (rĕf e rē´) — the person who enforces the rules of a game

scrimmage line (skrĭ´ mĭj līn) — in football, the imaginary line where two teams face each other before play begins

stadium (stā´ dē em) — a large structure where athletic games are played

synthetic (sĭn thĕt´ ĭk) — not found in nature; made by people

tackle (tăk´ el) — to knock down the player carrying the ball

time-out — to take a break from playing a game

touchdown (tŭch´ doun) — to get the ball over the goal line

INDEX

ABOUT THE AUTHOR

Ray Broekel is a full-time freelance writer who lives with his wife, Peg, and a dog, Fergus, in Ipswich, Massachusetts. He has had twenty years of experience as a children's book editor and newspaper supervisor, and has taught many subjects in kindergarten through college levels.

Dr. Broekel has had over 1,000 stories and articles published, and over 100 books. His first book was published in 1956 by Children's Press.